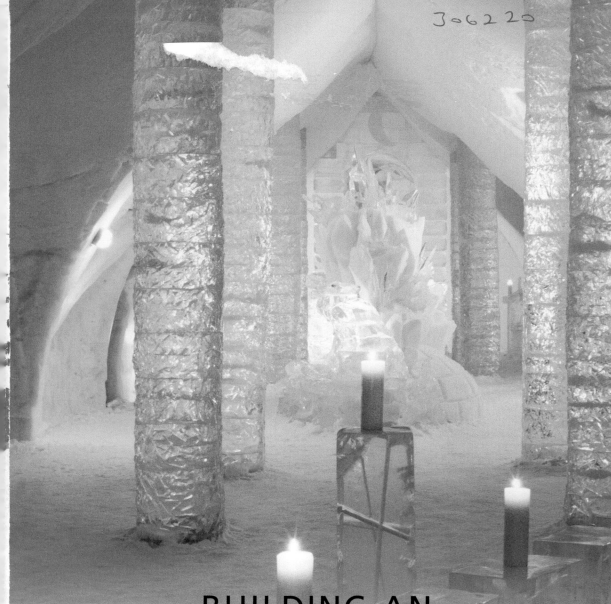

BUILDING AN
Ice Hotel

By Gib Goodfellow

Series Literacy Consultant
Dr Ros Fisher

Pearson Education Limited
Edinburgh Gate
Harlow
Essex CM20 2JE
England

www.longman.co.uk

ISBN 0 582 84122 4

Colour reproduction by Colourscan, Singapore
Printed and bound in China by Leo Paper Products Ltd.

The Publisher's policy is to use paper manufactured from sustainable forests.

10 9 8 7 6 5 4 3

The following people from **DK** have
contributed to the development of this product:

Art Director Rachael Foster

Martin Wilson **Managing Art Editor** | **Managing Editor** Marie Greenwood
Jane Tetzlaff **Design** | **Editorial** Hannah Wilson
Jo de Gray, Helen McFarland **Picture Research** | **Production** Gordana Simakovic
Richard Czapnik, Andy Smith **Cover Design** | **DTP** David McDonald

Consultant Jacques Desbois, CEO Ice Hotel Quebec-Canada Inc.

Dorling Kindersley would like to thank: Véronique Cyr and Marie-Noëlle Marceau at the Quebec Ice Hotel; David Glover for additional consultancy; Rose Horridge in the DK Picture Library; Ed Merrit for cartography; Kath Northam for additional design work; Mariana Sonnenburg for additional picture research; and Johnny Pau for additional cover design work.

Picture Credits: Alamy Images: Andre Jenny 10–11; Bryan and Cherry Alexander 4cl. Corbis: 23b; Nathan Benn 18bl; Perry Conway 26tc, 26tr, 26car; W. Geiersperger 8–9; Werner H. Müller 27tr; Anders Ryman 31tr; Randy M. Ury 26tl. Louis Ducharme: 1, 14–15, 17t, 20cr, 20–21. Duchesnay Station Touristique: 7tr. Getty Images: Wayne R. Bilenduke 24tl; Andre Gallant 3; Steve Kaufman 30b; Sebastien Starr 24–25; Pete Turner 28–29. Ice Hotel Quebec-Canada: 4cl, 6–7, 8tr, 10tr, 12br, 12t, 14tl; Xavier Dachez 16b. Jan Jordan: 4–5, 16tr, 17bl, 19b, 30tl. Masterfile UK: Freeman Patterson 21tr; Brian Sytnyk 25tr. National Geographic Image Collection: Roy Toft 27br. Rex Features: Norm Betts 13b, 19tr. Les Productions Tessima ltée: Yves Tessier 21bl. Woodfall Wild Images: Tom Murphy 26bl. Cover: Louis Ducharme: front t. Ice Hotel Quebec-Canada: front bl. Jan Jordan: back.

All other images: DK Dorling Kindersley © 2004. For further information see www.dkimages.com
Dorling Kindersley Ltd., 80 Strand, London WC2R ORL

Contents

A World of Ice

Jacques Desbois (JAHK day-BWAH) has always loved winter. He grew up in Quebec in Canada where winter lasts for many months and where Aboriginals have a long tradition of building igloos. Jacques' passion for snow led him to form a company that built igloos for festivals in Canada.

One day Jacques learned about a hotel in Sweden that was made of ice and snow. It seemed like a strange idea – the guests sleep on beds of ice, and when the temperature rises in the spring, the hotel melts away. Yet to a man who built igloos for a living, the idea of building such a hotel was an exciting challenge.

Jacques Desbois is so skilled in the construction of igloos and snow shelters that he is nicknamed "Mr Igloo".

The Ice Hotel in Sweden was the inspiration for Quebec's Ice Hotel.

Jacques went to Sweden to meet the hotel developers, and they explained to him how they had built their ice hotel. Jacques decided to try building his own in Quebec.

Back home two Canadian businessmen were looking for interesting new opportunities. They were excited by Jacques' project. The three men drew up plans and looked for more investors. Meanwhile, Jacques also investigated different techniques that could be used for building the hotel.

Soon several companies joined the project and provided equipment and money. Jacques and his partners borrowed money to buy more materials, more equipment and to employ workers.

Map Key

Major highway

Highway

River

Airport

Forest

Ice Hotel

Scale
0 miles 5   10   15
0 kilometres   15

Canada

Quebec City

United States

Lake St Joseph

2nd Ice Hotel

1st Ice Hotel

Quebec City

Montmorency River

N
W — E
S

Jacques-Cartier River

St Lawrence River

Quebec City sits on the banks of the Saint Lawrence River in eastern Canada. The first two ice hotels were built near the city.

Jacques Desbois wanted to build the Ice Hotel close to Quebec City for three reasons. First Quebec City has winters cold enough to keep an ice hotel frozen for several months. Second Jacques and his partners lived there, and it would be easier for them to oversee the project. Third Jacques knew he could find enough people in Quebec City to build and run the Ice Hotel.

In December 2000 Jacques built his first ice hotel at Montmorency Falls, just north east of Quebec City. It had space for twenty-two guests. The grand opening in January 2001 was covered by many newspapers and television stations. Guests came from all over the world to visit the Ice Hotel.

Jacques and his partners built a second hotel in the winter of 2002. This hotel was built in the Duchesnay Ecotourism Station, north west of Quebec City. It was situated on more than 142 square kilometres of forest and had thirteen lakes. Guests were to stay one night in the Ice Hotel and other nights in the resort's cabins and lodges. They were to eat in the resort's restaurant and enjoy all the outdoor activities available at the site.

The cabins and lodges of the Duchesnay Ecotourism Station are found in the countryside that surrounds Quebec City.

Jacques and his team chose a site beside Lake Saint Joseph which is the largest of the thirteen lakes. They needed a large, flat area and plenty of water to make snow. This site was perfect.

The water used to make the snow for the second Ice Hotel came from Lake Saint Joseph.

Building Begins

In July 2001 work started on the new Ice Hotel. First architects started work on the designs. Then the engineers checked the plans to make sure that the building would be safe.

In early December 2001 before much snow had fallen, the workers prepared the building site. Timber and steel arrived. These would be made into moulds and frames for the Ice Hotel walls. Tractors and other heavy equipment for moving the building materials and the snow were brought to the site.

Workers at the building site followed the architects' plans closely.

Why does water expand when it freezes?

Water is one of the only substances on Earth that expands when it freezes. This expansion occurs because the water particles move farther apart as the water reaches its freezing point (0˚C).

plastic bottle full of water

bottle bursts when water turns to ice and expands

Everything was ready to start, but there was not enough snow to make the hotel. There was only about one month left to finish in time for the opening. The workers couldn't wait for nature to deliver snow. They had to make their own.

As soon as the temperature fell to −5°C, water was pumped out of the freezing Lake Saint Joseph into three snow-making machines. These machines sprayed a fine mist of water that froze quickly in the cold air.

Snow-making machines spray water which freezes to form snow if the air is cold enough.

The compacted snow that was created by the machines was perfect for building. In total, the builders needed to make more than 10,000 tonnes of compacted snow.

Snow is a wonderful building material. It is simple to move, very strong and is easy to shape into beautiful patterns.

Snow-making machines created mounds of snow for the walls of the hotel.

Three forms of water: solid, liquid and gas

Water is made up of tiny particles or molecules. The way the molecules are arranged and move about depends on whether the water is in solid, liquid or gas form.

Ice (solid) molecules

Water (liquid) molecules

Water vapour (gas) molecules

Molecules in solids are arranged in a regular structure. Each molecule can vibrate but cannot move far. Solids, such as ice, have a fixed shape.

Molecules in liquids are not arranged in a regular structure. They can move about freely. Liquids, such as water, don't have a fixed shape.

Molecules in gases are more widely spaced than molecules in liquids. They move quickly and spread to fill the shape of their container.

Jacques knew that the snow would act like a blanket to help insulate the building because warm air gets trapped between snowflakes. Moving air carries heat away very quickly, but the tiny pockets of trapped air inside a layer of snow help block the flow of heat.

Most buildings have a frame of wood or steel onto which the walls and roof are attached. Building the Ice Hotel, however, was more like building with concrete. Moulds are used with concrete buildings to keep the concrete in place until it hardens. Then the moulds are removed.

The next step for the team was to make the moulds that would determine the shape of the hotel. The moulds would keep the snow in place until it hardened.

How do snowflakes form?

Snowflakes are a collection of tiny snow crystals. Crystals, such as those shown below, form when the water vapour in clouds freezes. Snow crystals may fall to the ground as they are, or they may stick together with other crystals to form large snowflakes. Snow crystals usually have six sides, and no two snowflakes are exactly alike.

Moulds were put in place before being covered in snow.

Workers constructed metal arches to act as the moulds. The arches had cross braces to support the weight of the snow. Then tractors moved the steel moulds into position. The moulds had ski-like runners along their edges to allow them to be moved more easily. Then snow was blown over the moulds to form ceilings and walls. Finally the snow had to freeze which took from ten to seventy-two hours.

Snow covered the moulds and froze to form ice.

After the snow hardened, everyone watched anxiously as the workers carefully removed the moulds. When the last one was removed, the team breathed a sigh of relief. The walls were strong and solid. They were more than 45 centimetres thick at the highest point and twice as thick at the bottom. Jacques had used this design to make sure the base would be strong enough to support the weight of the ceiling.

Workers added interior walls to divide the spaces into guest rooms. Then they removed the wooden frames that were used to create the doorways and hung curtains across the open spaces. Without real doors, there was no way to lock the guest rooms. Guests would have to leave their valuables in another building.

Why use arches?

load

blocks pressed together tightly by load

A flat roof is weak. The load in the middle makes it bend down, pulling the blocks apart at the joins. However, when the blocks are built in a curved arch, the load squeezes them together more tightly. This makes the arch shape incredibly strong.

Finally, the moulds were pulled out by tractors. They slid out easily on their ski-like runners.

13

Ice blocks came from Montreal. They were used for the construction of interior walls, pillars and furniture.

Finally, all that was needed to complete the structure of the Ice Hotel was ice. Crystal-clear blocks of ice made from purified water were delivered to the site. Workers used the blocks to make walls at the ends of some sections of the hotel. These walls were strong and added to the beauty of the Ice Hotel.

The ice walls were not just for decoration. They also let in natural light which was important. Few electric lights were used because light bulbs produce heat which would raise the temperature inside the hotel and melt the ice. Still, every room was wired with electricity that passed along waterproof cables hidden in the walls, floors and ceilings of the hotel.

The external structure of the Quebec Ice Hotel was finished. However, there was still a lot of work to be done on the inside of the hotel before the guests arrived.

Finishing Touches

The structure of the Ice Hotel was complete, with sturdy walls and an elegant design. However, with no decorations, it seemed a little bare. It was time to decorate the interior.

Technicians started work on the Grand Hall first. This would be the first room guests would see. Skilled workers made ice columns from blocks to help support the roof. These columns also added a decorative touch. Artists created ice sculptures and decorated the walls with carvings. Finally, the walls were polished to make them smooth and shiny.

A chandelier made of ice hung in the Grand Hall.

This room is where food and drinks were served in the first Quebec Ice Hotel in 2001.

Drinks were served in glasses made of ice.

Near the Grand Hall was a large room with tables and chairs carved from ice and a long ice counter where drinks and food were served. Smoked meats and fish were served to guests on plates of ice. Even the glasses used to serve drinks were carved from ice. Of course, guests did not need ice cubes, but they probably needed gloves.

A theatre near the Grand Hall had room to seat more than twenty guests. The films, which all had snow and ice as a theme, were projected onto a wall of pure white snow.

The Iroquois people made rattles from turtle shells. They filled the shells with pebbles and added a wooden handle.

The Ice Hotel also included two exhibition rooms where guests could view artefacts of the Aboriginal people of Canada. Canada was home to the Iroquois, Algonquins and Inuit long before European settlers arrived in North America. For the 2002 season the exhibition was devoted to the Iroquois.

Before the hotel officially opened, the people of the Iroquois Nation arrived with historical artefacts to display. They decorated the exhibition room to look like the inside of their ancestors' wood and bark longhouses. First they placed a frame of wooden poles inside the room. Next they built beds along the walls. Then they made storage shelves above the beds. Finally they hung corn, animal pelts and tools from the wooden poles, just as their ancestors would have done. Although the walls of the exhibition were ice, and not bark, guests got an idea of what it was like to live in a longhouse.

Up to twelve Iroquois families lived inside each longhouse. This is a reconstruction of a longhouse.

Maize cobs were gathered in baskets, then hung to dry in the longhouses.

18

In the second exhibition room were ice sculptures, including those of two herons, a salmon and a statue of Hector de Saint-Denys Garneau – one of the greatest poets of Quebec. Ice for these sculptures had to be specially made from purified water to ensure that it was crystal clear to reflect the light.

A sculptor at the Ice Hotel used a chainsaw to carve an ice model of an Inuit inside an igloo.

Magnificent ice thrones were sculpted for the hotel.

In every guest room was an ice bed. Ice slabs with lights formed the bases of the beds. Wooden boxes set on the bases kept the guests comfortably off the ice. A foam cushion and deerskins covered the boxes. Guests were also given warm sleeping bags and pillows.

A bathroom caravan was connected to the hallway. The trailer contained a toilet, a sink and, happily for the guests, an electric heater. Guests could prepare for bed and get dressed in the morning in comfort.

Fireplaces added a cheerful glow to some guest rooms. They were specially designed not to produce heat which would melt the walls.

The heated trailer was the warmest place in the hotel. Everywhere else the temperature was between –5 and –2°C. That's just below the temperature at which water freezes (0°C).

Outside the hotel were grounds where people could meet to have bonfires and fireworks. There were also hot tubs for soaking and splashing. Next to the tubs were mounds of fresh snow. Brave guests could take a "snow bath" by rolling in the snow before jumping into the hot tubs.

Why does ice look blue?

Light is made up of light particles called photons. They are different colours, depending on how much energy they have. Red and orange photons have less energy than blue photons. Pure ice is almost completely transparent. Most photons travel right through it. However, some photons are completely absorbed by ice molecules. More red and orange photons are absorbed than blue, so the remaining light has a blue tint. This is why ice looks blue when it transmits or reflects light.

The guests at the Ice Hotel were treated to firework displays at night.

Exploring a Frozen World

On 15th January 2002 the first guests arrived at the Ice Hotel. During the day, the guests were busy outdoors. There was so much to do. Guests could go hiking, cross-country skiing or ice skating. They could travel about on dogsleds or snowmobiles. They could go ice fishing or learn the history of the fur trade. They could also learn about the wildlife in the forests around them.

Ice skating was popular. Jacques had included an unusual skating rink that was half indoors and half outdoors. Guests could glide about in the sparkling sunshine, then skate back inside to the snack bar for a cup of hot chocolate.

How do skates work?

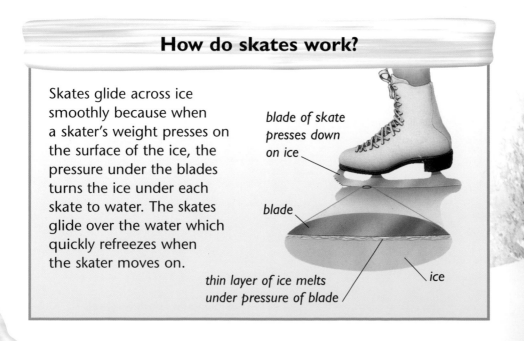

Skates glide across ice smoothly because when a skater's weight presses on the surface of the ice, the pressure under the blades turns the ice under each skate to water. The skates glide over the water which quickly refreezes when the skater moves on.

blade of skate presses down on ice

blade

thin layer of ice melts under pressure of blade

ice

Guests who chose to hike found that the snow around the Ice Hotel was packed down neatly. In the woods, however, the snow was nearly 60 centimetres deep, so guests had to lift their feet high enough to walk. Many people wore snowshoes which kept them on top of the snow and made walking more comfortable. The guests followed a trail that covered more than 10 kilometres around the Ice Hotel.

Aboriginal snowshoes consist of netting attached to frames.

During the 2002 season, the most popular activity at the hotel was cross-country skiing. Guests skied on more than 145 kilometres of trails. They stopped at heated huts along the ski trails to rest and have a hot drink.

(!) Winter sports can be dangerous. Never ski or hike outdoors without an experienced guide.

Guests tried ice fishing from heated fishing shacks on the frozen lake. Guests sat in the shacks and put their fishing lines into the water through holes cut in the ice. They chatted and relaxed while they waited for the fish to take the bait.

Other guests explored the far corners of the resort area by dogsled. A musher, who cared for the dogs and the sleds, met the guests at the hotel.

Inuit people sometimes use harpoons to fish. Guests at the Ice Hotel used an easier method – fishing lines.

Two or three people sat on the sled beneath deerskins which kept them warm. The musher ran behind the sled and jumped on when the dogs ran faster. He called out directions to the lead dog who turned left or right on command.

Another popular activity at the Ice Hotel was snowmobiling. Guests sped along the trails on frozen Lake Saint Joseph. They wore special snowmobile suits to keep them warm. Helmets with windshields protected their faces from the cold and wet.

Huskies are excellent sled dogs. They have thick, warm fur and move quickly over great distances.

Many guests enjoyed snowmobiling, but the noise of the vehicles scared away wildlife.

Snow preserves a record of recent animal movement.

Guests at the hotel learned how sap is collected from maple trees to make syrup.

Many guests also wanted to learn more about the forest around the Ice Hotel. Skilled guides took them out on snowshoes to learn about the different trees and plants. Guides also told the guests about the history of the local timber industry. They showed them tools used by the lumberjacks. Guests learned how to make maple syrup and sugar from maple tree sap.

The red fox can adapt to habitats as different as city parks and the snow and ice of the Arctic.

Some guests chose to learn about wildlife in the forest. Fur was found where a moose had scratched its hide on a tree. Piles of feathers showed that a hawk had just had dinner. Deer and moose were occasionally seen, but often the smaller animals, such as minks and weasels, left only their footprints in the snow.

At night, there was an owl outing. First a guide told the guests about the great grey owl which is found in the surrounding forest. Then the guide told the guests how and where to spot one. Finally he led the guests out into the snowy woods to look for the great grey owl.

The great grey owl can plunge into snow to catch its prey.

The moose is the largest member of the deer family.

The Season Ends

At the end of March, the hotel staff said goodbye to the last guests and prepared to close the Ice Hotel. Supplies such as deerskins, bed boards, lights and wires were removed and put in storage for next year. The bathroom caravan was towed away.

When only ice and snow remained, the hotel was ready for destruction. Workers drove huge machines over the top of the Ice Hotel. In only five hours, the machines destroyed what had taken five weeks to build. The Ice Hotel was gone, with the ice and snow that had been used to construct it now part of the wintry Quebec landscape.

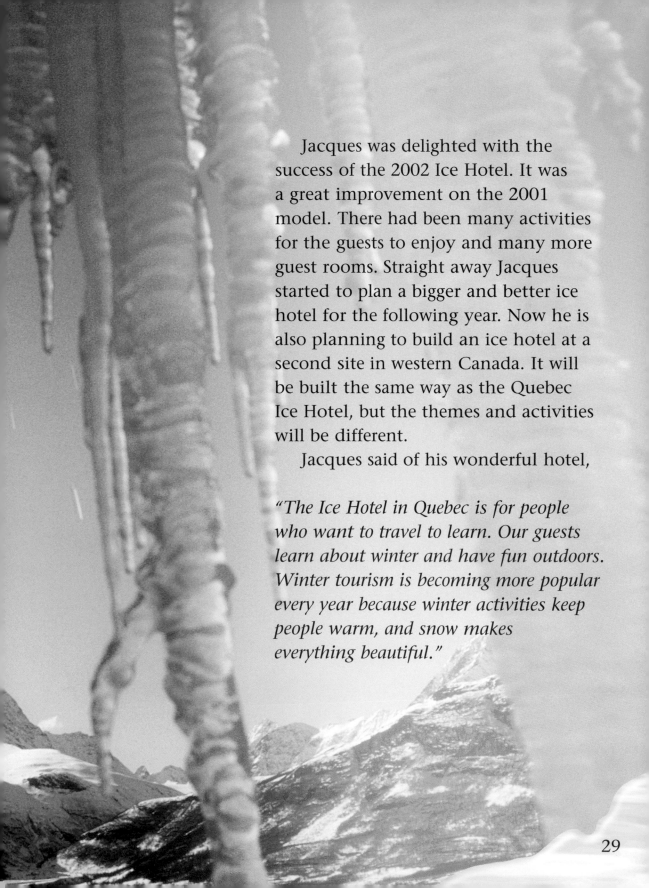

Jacques was delighted with the success of the 2002 Ice Hotel. It was a great improvement on the 2001 model. There had been many activities for the guests to enjoy and many more guest rooms. Straight away Jacques started to plan a bigger and better ice hotel for the following year. Now he is also planning to build an ice hotel at a second site in western Canada. It will be built the same way as the Quebec Ice Hotel, but the themes and activities will be different.

Jacques said of his wonderful hotel,

"The Ice Hotel in Quebec is for people who want to travel to learn. Our guests learn about winter and have fun outdoors. Winter tourism is becoming more popular every year because winter activities keep people warm, and snow makes everything beautiful."

Ice Adventures Around the World

A fishing trip in a boat made of ice is one adventure visitors to Sweden won't forget.

Visitors to Japan's Snow and Ice Festival enjoy an ice slide.

Today there are ice hotels in other countries. In Greenland, the Igloo Village Hotel is a collection of igloo-like domes of snow that are connected by snow passageways and lit by candles. Finland also has an Igloo Village in Kakslauttanen (kak-slow-TAH-nen). Guests can visit a reindeer farm and learn about the Saami – the native people of Scandinavia.

Hotels are not the only places where snow and ice are celebrated. A festival in Sapporo, Japan, is dedicated to ice and snow. Every February, the city is transformed with ice sculptures and structures. There are huge carvings of gods and goddesses, palaces and even the pyramids of Egypt.

In northern Sweden, there is a two-storey theatre made of snow and ice. At night, spectators sit on reindeer skins which cover the icy seats to watch performances by Saami actors. During the interval, the spectators have a warm drink and gaze up at the stars above, as the theatre has no roof. Every springtime, the theatre melts, but every winter it is rebuilt for another season.

These Saami actors are performing on a stage made of ice.

Snow and ice are not only enjoyed in cold countries. Ice sculptors create magnificent ice sculptures for displays in hotels and restaurants in many parts of the world, not just the Ice Hotel in Canada. All an ice sculptor needs is a large fridge to stop the sculpture melting before it goes on display.

Matsumura is an ice sculptor from Japan. He carves a swan for a hotel display.

Index

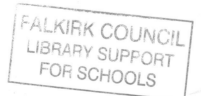